JESUS IS ALL YOU NEED

A STUDY IN COLOSSIANS

BY MIKE LEAKE

Illustrated by Ed Koehler

Cover design and interior layout by Dawn Lamper

DEDICATION

TO ISAIAH AND HANNAH, MAY YOUR LIVES AND YOUR SMILES
TESTIFY TO THE INFINITE WORTH OF JESUS.

TABLE OF CONTENTS

FOREWORD

Professor Jamie Smith was once asked by a college student about what steps he should take if he wanted to be a great theologian one day. "That's easy," Smith replied. "Go teach fifth-grade Sunday School."

There's something beautiful in that piece of advice, something that bursts the pretentious bubble of our theological discourse and brings us back down to earth, to the rough and tumble theology relevant to the kid who wants to play dodge ball, the girl who loves to read, the boy who's obsessed with Minecraft, and the kid down the street who is setting up a lemonade stand.

The mark of expertly teaching God's Word is not mastering all the intricacies of Greek and Hebrew, in order to startle people with your wonderful knowledge. It's to lovingly translate God's Word into a language a child can understand, to gently explain the truths of God's Word—not shying away from the hard passages or glossing over the difficult sections, but carefully considering how best to bring home God's truth to a little child's heart.

Mike Leake is passionate about theology, not to impress his children with his own expertise, but to help them understand God's Word and come to know God. The

Seeds Project has been forged in the fire of evening devotions, those moments of mayhem when the world is winding down and your children are getting out their last bursts of energy. Everything about these devotions, from the illustrations to the memorable analogies, from their brevity (thank you, Lord!) to their engaging activities, demonstrates the hands-on experience of someone who says, "I'm trying this to see what works with my kids."

> " The Seeds Project has been forged in the fire of evening devotions, those moments of mayhem when the world is winding down and your children are getting out their last bursts of energy.

As a writer and editor for the Gospel Project, as someone who is passionate about seeing kids learn Bible stories and how they connect to Christ, I'm excited to see Mike's labor of love come into fruition. I hope these devotionals will help kids learn how to navigate a challenging and often intimidating book like the Bible. But most of all, I pray that through these pages, kids will come to know Christ - the Hero of the Bible, the One who saves and sanctifies and who will make all things new.

TREVIN WAX
AUTHOR, MANAGING EDITOR OF THE GOSPEL PROJECT

SPECIAL THANKS

This project would have never left the ground without our generous Kickstarter backers. You'll never know the seeds that you've planted because of your gracious support. Thank you for believing in this project.

I also want to thank all of the tremendous parents and children that gave some of these devotions a test run. You helped encourage me to continue on with the project and your suggestions were vital in making this the project that it is today.

Finally, thanks to all of the kind editors, illustrators, and graphic designers that made this project what it is today. Without your efforts we would have jumbled words, illustrated by stick figures, and distributed on papyrus sheets. Thank you.

INTRODUCTION

When my son turned five, my wife and I went to the nearest book store and bought him his first Bible. I also wanted a good devotional that we could read together as a family to help us understand the Bible. There were a few things that were decent, but nothing that really fit what we were looking for.

What we were really looking for was a devotional that would go through one book of the Bible at a time. And one that would train our children how to do Bible study. Of course, I also wanted it to be engaging and easy enough to actually maintain. In my mind the best resource would be one that helped us as parents to disciple our kids. It'd be full enough that on busy nights we could simply read it together, but it'd also be open ended enough that we could have great discussions as a family.

I couldn't find what I was looking for in the store and so I decided to write my own. I wrote about twenty devotions on Paul's letter to the Colossians, took it to Staples, and turned it into a little devotional for my son and gave it to him for his birthday.

After going through these devotions with my own son and listening to the frustrations of other parents I decided to work towards making this curriculum available to other parents. I've tweaked it to make it relevant for girls as well as boys. And I've given sample devotions to other parents to get their child's feedback.

> "...continue in what you have learned and have firmly believed, knowing from whom you learned it..."

I also knew that I needed to make the project aesthetically pleasing to both parents and children. Because my artistic talent extends to stick figures and butterflies, I partnered with Ed Koehler and Dawn Lamper to make the devotionals fun and attractive. I am confident that you will agree with me that they have done a tremendous job in making The Seeds Project beautiful.

You will also notice that The Seeds Project is written in colloquial language. That is another way of saying that it's written in the informal way that we talk to one another. It is also written on such a level that most beginning readers should be able to read it with just a little assistance from adults.

Occasionally you'll come across words or concepts in this devotional that might be difficult for kids to comprehend. Truthfully, this is one of the reasons that I desired to write a devotional that walks through one book of the Bible. It pushes us to deal with the whole counsel of God and not just the easy stuff. I want to see families (including my own) wrestling through difficult texts in the Bible. I want children to be exposed to—and learn to surrender to—the whole counsel of God's Word. There is value in helping our children know they don't have to understand everything.

In 2 Timothy 3:14, the apostle Paul charges Timothy to "continue in what you have learned and have firmly believed, knowing from whom you learned it..." Paul assumes that a foundation has been built in Timothy's life. Verse 15 tells us where that foundation was built, as Paul goes on to say, "...and how from childhood you have been acquainted with the sacred writings". That is the goal of The Seeds Project. In the same way that Timothy's mother and grandmother had planted the sacred writings into him—I want to see parents plant gospel seeds into the hearts of their children. I believe that this is best done as we wrestle together through one book of Scripture at a time. That is why we've created The Seeds Project.

I don't want to pretend that this is going to be easy. This is difficult work. But it is worth it. In 2 Timothy 3:15, there is a precious truth that keeps me going as I labor to plant gospel seeds into the heart of my own children. As Paul refers to those sacred writings that Timothy's mother and grandmother labored to impart to young Timothy, he says this about them, "[they] are able to make you wise for salvation through faith in Jesus Christ". The gospel seeds that you and I plant through God's Word are the means that God uses to bring our children to faith in the Lord. It is hard work—but it's worth every drop of sweat.

So enjoy this labor of love with your children as God uses his word to the Colossians to plant gospel seeds into your little one.

WHO ARE THE COLOSSIANS?

Colossians was written by a guy named Paul to a church at a place called Colossae. When you read a book in the Bible it is important to know who wrote the book and why he wrote it. It is also helpful to know who the book was written to. So, we are going to learn a little about the Colossians.

The first people to read this letter lived a long time ago. If they were somehow still alive today, they would be almost 2,000 years old. They also spoke a different language than we speak. They would have spoken a language called Greek. But even though they lived so far away, so long ago, and spoke a different language, they were people just like you and me. And they were people who had a hard time believing Jesus was all that they needed.

Field Notes

》 LOOK UP A MAP OF COLOSSAE*

》 NEXT, GO TO HOWMANYMILES.ORG AND TYPE IN THE PLACE WHERE YOU LIVE AND THEN TYPE IN COLOSSAE, TURKEY.

》 HOW MANY MILES AWAY IS COLOSSAE?

The Colossian people were really scared of things like monsters. And they believed that if you followed the rules, then the monsters would be happy. But if you didn't follow the rules, the monsters would get mad. Some of the Colossians wore

*You can find a good map of Colossae here: http://bit.ly/1emLvN9.

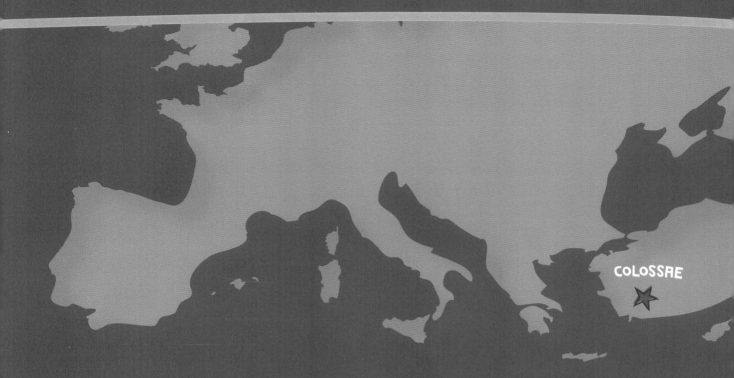

magic crystals around their necks to keep the evil monsters away and to make the good monsters their friends. Paul wrote his letter to them to help them understand that Jesus is greater than everything. Even the scariest monster (which didn't exist) is nothing compared to Jesus. And even the coolest monster in the world is nothing compared to Jesus.

We do this same thing today. We might not be afraid of things like monsters but we can be scared of other things. What things are you afraid of?

How is Jesus stronger than the things you are scared of?

WOW! COLOSSAE IS FAR AWAY!

The message to the Colossians (and to us) is that Jesus is all that we need. Let's pray and thank God for giving us Jesus because he is all that we need.

THANKING GOD FOR OTHER PEOPLE

LET'S SHARE SOME THINGS THAT WE ARE THANKFUL FOR.

PAPERTOWEL
JESUSCROSS

Paul had a thanksgiving list too. One of the things on that list was how God was working in the life of the Colossians. Paul knew that there are certain things that only God can do. Only God can cause people to have faith and love in their lives. So, when Paul saw that his friends had faith and love in their lives, he knew that it was God working in their hearts. This is why he thanked God for them.

What are things that only God can do?

What are ways that God is working in your friends and family?

_____

_____

_____

The work of God that I'm thankful for are:

_____

_____

_____

Pick two people that you know. Take some time thanking God for how he is working in their lives. Now continue praying for them by asking God to continue his work in their life. How is God working in your life?

HOPE LAID UP IN HEAVEN

Do you remember why Paul had to write this letter to the Colossians? They were scared that things like that could take away what was most special to them. And what was most special to them was Jesus. They thought that these scary things could take away their place in heaven. But Paul wrote to them to remind them that their "hope is laid up in heaven". What that means is that Jesus is keeping their place in heaven to be with him someday. Their hope is safe—which means that it can't be broken, and it can't be lost.

Some things in our life are temporary. Temporary means that it will not last forever. The food you ate was temporary. The television is temporary. What are other things that are temporary?

Some things in life are eternal. Eternal means that it will last forever. Jesus is eternal. Love is eternal. Our souls are eternal. What are other things that are eternal?

Jim Elliott was a man that gave up temporary things so that he could tell people about Jesus. He actually died telling people

Field Notes

> IT IS REALLY SAD WHEN THINGS WE LOVE GET BROKEN OR WHEN WE BUILD SOMETHING COOL AND SOMEONE BREAKS IT. THOSE THINGS CAN BE REALLY SAD.

> THE WORST TOY THAT I'VE BROKEN OR LOST:

about Jesus. One time he wrote in his journal:

> ## "He is no fool who gives what he cannot keep to gain what he cannot lose."

The people that he was telling about Jesus didn't know that Jim was there to help them. But Jim knew that because these people had souls that would live forever. He wanted them to live forever with Jesus and so he did whatever it took to tell them the message of Jesus.

Sadly, these people had evil hearts and so they decided to kill Jim and his friends instead of listening to his message. But Jim knew that telling them about Jesus was even more important than his own life. He gave up what was temporary (his life and all of his stuff) because he knew that things that last forever are more important.

Eventually, these people came to know Jesus. Jim's wife, Elisabeth, visited them again and continued to share the good news of Jesus with them. This time, they came to know Jesus, and their lives were changed forever.

Only those who trust in Jesus with their lives have eternal life.

What in your life is temporary? What is eternal? Which one matters the most?

GOSPEL GROWING

COLOSSIANS 1:5B-8

MAKE A LIST OF ALL THE
PEOPLE THAT HAVE TOLD
YOU THE GOSPEL.

_____

_____

_____

_____

_____

In 2009, many people were afraid of something that was called the pig flu. It didn't turn you into a pig, but it made people really sick. Some people even died. It was in the news every day. Not every sickness makes it to the TV, only the really bad ones. The pig flu made it to TV.

In order for a sickness like this to be anything to catch our attention, two things have to happen. First, it has to be contagious. Do you know what contagious means? It means that you can give it to somebody else. If it isn't contagious, then only one poor guy will get it. The pig flu was very contagious. Secondly, it has to make you very sick. Otherwise who cares if you only sneeze a couple times? It won't make the news unless it changes the way that you live. When people got the pig flu, they were so tired and sick that they stayed in bed all the time. They couldn't leave the house either.

You are probably wondering why we are talking about the pig flu. Let me tell you. It's actually a picture of how the gospel spreads. The gospel is the good news of Jesus taking away our sins and giving us a relationship with him.

This would be a good time for you to share your personal testimony with your child.

Guess what? All of the people on your list has a list of other people who shared the gospel with them*. And you know what? Those people have a list too. In fact, if we could trace them all the way back, the reason why we have heard the gospel is because of the faithfulness of someone telling the story of Jesus to someone else. In verse 6, Paul says that the gospel has "come to you". That's a word that means "snuggling up to". The good news of Jesus has snuggled up to the hearts of the believers at Colossae. Then Paul tells them how that happened.

IT LOOKED LIKE THIS:

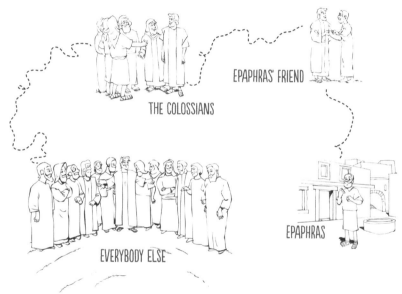

EPAPHRAS' FRIEND

THE COLOSSIANS

EVERYBODY ELSE

EPAPHRAS

This story helps us to see that in order for the story of Jesus to spread to the world, it has to be treasured by the people who hear it. And then it has to be shared by the people who treasure it.

Do you treasure the story of Jesus?

Who can you share this treasure with?

KNOWLEDGE OF GOD
That Makes Your Heart Break-dance!

In these verses, Paul was praying for the Colossians. The first thing that Paul prayed for was that the Colossians would know God in such a way that it would make their hearts and souls do a break dance.

There are different types of knowledge. There is one type that is called head knowledge. For example, answer this question:

Who was the first president of the United States?

_____

I bet you got that right. If you didn't it was George Washington. Now to learn about the second type of knowledge, see if you can answer this question:

You don't know the answer to that, do you? We might be able to guess that it smelled a little funny because some of his teeth were wooden, and some of his teeth came from animals. **GROSS!** You can't answer that question because you do not have what is called personal knowledge of George Washington. But can you answer this question?

What does my breath smell like?

Hopefully you didn't say moldy French cheese. **YUCK!** Regardless of what you said, you were able to answer it because you know me. That is what it means to have personal knowledge of someone. There is a difference between knowing about someone and actually knowing someone. You know me, and I know you.

It is this second type of knowledge that is the prayer in verse 10. It is a prayer that we might truly know God and that we would know God in such a way that it makes our heart break-dance. To really know God is to treasure him above all else. And we see from verse 10 that such knowledge of God actually changes your life. It makes you "walk in a manner worthy of the Lord". That means to live in such a way that everybody knows what your treasure is.

What would people say your treasure is? What do you think my greatest treasures are? Pray this prayer (Col. 1:9-12) for yourself. Pick a few people and pray this for them, too.

JOYFULLY ENDURING WITH GOD'S POWER

COLOSSIANS 1:9-12

Today we get to look at being really strong. Let's begin by watching a few YouTube videos of some really strong people. *

WOW! Do you think you could lift those things? Do you think mom or dad could lift them? What do you think those guys had to do to be able to lift such heavy things? Did it take lots of practice and pain for them to be able to lift such heavy stuff? I bet they had to eat a bunch of healthy foods too, and probably not very much soda and candy. It takes a ton of effort to have so much power.

But guess what? None of those guys comes close to having as much power as God does! Not a single one of those guys can stand before a grave and say, "Lazarus come forth!" and then see the very dead Lazarus come walking out of the grave.** None of them can take our hearts and say, "Let there be light". None of them can create the world simply by speaking.

The type of power that God is talking about here isn't big muscles. It's the power to do hard things. What are some of the really hard things that you have to do in your life?

*Simply go to YouTube and type in World's Strongest Man Highlights. Be sure to sample these beforehand.
**If you haven't already shared the story of Jesus and Lazarus (John 11), this is a good time.

When you get older, things sometimes get even more difficult. God sometimes calls us to do really hard things. Doing hard things means that we do things for other people when we'd rather do things for ourselves. It also means being faithful to Jesus when it costs us a great deal. Sometimes we really want to do things that God doesn't want us to do. We need God's power to remain faithful.

Notice one last word from these verses. In verse 11, Paul uses the word joy. Do you know what joy means? It means being happy, content, and rested even when things are really tough. Did you know that it takes God's power for us to have joy? Joy is a gift from God.

Thank God for his power. Pray for his power to be faithful to Jesus. What are a few things that you need God's power for in your life right now?

LIVING A LIFE OF THANKS

Most people wouldn't pick this guy for their baseball team. We often pick people based upon how they look. If they look big and strong and athletic we pick them first for our team. The guy in this picture doesn't look like he would be very good at baseball so he would probably get picked last.

It can be painful to be the person who is always picked last. It hurts when people don't pick us for teams or don't want to play with us. It's also frustrating when we stand in line to ride a roller coaster only to find out that we aren't big enough to ride it yet. Whether it's not being picked for a team or not being able to ride roller coasters, we don't like to be left out. The word for that is "disqualified". It means that you don't have what it takes to get the prize.

The Colossians had a similar problem. They were being told by a group of bad teachers that they were disqualified in the eyes of God. They were told that God wasn't going to pick them for his kingdom because they didn't do the right things to make him happy. The people at Colossae were tricked into believing that God had somehow disqualified them. That is why these words from Paul would have made them very happy:

"...giving thanks to the Father,
who has qualified you...."

Qualified—what a beautiful word! It means that these Colossians have God's attention. They can come into his presence and pray to him anytime they want. It means that they "have what it takes" to be in a relationship with God.

How do you think they came about "having what it takes" to be a part of God's special kingdom? It wasn't through what they did. It wasn't through their own efforts or because they tried really hard to be good and do good things. They are accepted into God's kingdom because of what Jesus has done for them. As we will read next time in verse 13-14, they are qualified because God has "delivered them" and "transferred them into Jesus' kingdom". They are qualified because God made them qualified. How awesome is that? And for that they will forever give thanks.

Why should we always give God thanks for His gospel of Jesus?

Only those who trust in (treasure) Jesus are qualified. Have you been rescued by Jesus? How does being qualified by God make a difference when we are disappointed?

JESUS IS THE GREATEST HERO

One of the reasons we like superheroes is because we like stories of rescue. Sometimes we think of ourselves as being the superhero coming to rescue helpless people. At other times, something within us realizes that we are the ones who need rescuing. The truth is, you don't have to be a superhero to rescue people. There are everyday heroes all around us.

When your house is on fire, who is the hero?

_____

When you need protection from a bad guy, who is the hero?

_____

Field Notes

❯ MY FAVORITE SUPERHERO IS:

When you fall down and need a band-aid, a glass of milk, or to find a toy you lost who is the hero?

_____

Someday, someone else might need you to be their hero. We all have to play the role of hero sometimes. But none of us, not even our favorite superheroes, are heroes like Jesus.

Colossians 1:13 says that through Jesus, God delivered us from the land of darkness. Are you ever afraid of the dark? Can you imagine living in a land where there is nothing but darkness all the time? That is what "land of darkness" means. And this is what the Bible says our hearts are like without Jesus. God has rescued us from this terrible kingdom and put us into the wonderful and beautiful kingdom of Jesus.

This rescue is much bigger than anything Spider-man or Batman or any of the Avengers could do for us. Because the enemy that Jesus rescues us from is more powerful than any other enemy these good guys have faced. This enemy is what makes all of the bad guys bad guys. It's an evil that is within all of our hearts. This evil is what we call "sin."

God tells us in the Bible that the wages of sin is death. That means that sin leads to death. We need forgiveness from sin. That is what Jesus does. He rescues us from our sins. Jesus is mighty to save us from our sins. He is a bigger superhero than any of these other guys because they all have sin and cannot rescue us from sin. But Jesus has never sinned, so he can rescue us from sin and all its effects. Jesus is our greatest hero.

What do you need to be rescued from?

Thank Jesus for being our hero.

27

WHY IS THAT STAR THERE?

COLOSSIANS 1:15-17

THIS IS A FUN SITE FOR VIEWING CONSTELLATIONS: HTTP://BIT.LY/89SSG1

Go outside and look at the stars. Try to find as many constellations as you can.* Now let's get on the Internet and look at a few of the different planets. How are they different?

How is Jupiter different from the other planets?

_____

_____

How is Saturn different from the other planets?

_____

_____

How is the Earth different from the other planets?

_____

Be prepared for this lesson by either bookmarking a few pictures of Jupiter, Saturn, and Earth. Also bookmark a few pictures of different people. If you'd prefer not to use the Internet to search for pictures of people then be prepared with photos of many different friends and family members.

Now let's look at a couple of pictures on the Internet. Let's pick a couple different people to look up. How are all of these people different? What is different about you compared to some of these other people?

So many things in God's creation are different. Planets are different. Stars are different. People are different. Why is that? What makes things different? Why is that star there and not over there at another place? Why is Saturn next to Jupiter and not right next to the Earth?

The simple—yet HUGE—answer to all of this is because Jesus wanted it that way. That is one of the things that this verse means. It means that everything was created by Jesus (That means he drew up the plan.) It was created through Jesus (that means that he was the carpenter who built it.) It was created for Jesus (it was for his glory that these things were created the way they were.) He was also before all things and in him all things hold together (that means that Jesus is the one who keeps us from flying off into outer space.) What keeps our hearts beating is Jesus. Maybe this is another reason why Jesus is the greatest hero.

Thank God for his unique creation.

How does this help the way that we look at other people?

What does it mean for your life that you were created for Jesus?

COLOSSIANS 1:18-20

Last time we talked about how everybody is different. Today we are going to use a magnet and a few paper clips to show something beautiful about what Jesus does through his gospel.

Let's make up three different people. You pick who they are and let's tell stories about them. Let's talk about the things that they like and the things they don't like. Let's talk about how they are totally different people.

PERSON A

Now I will use a paper clip for each one of these people. The magnet will represent Jesus. (I know that's kind of silly.) But what happens in the gospel is that Jesus draws people to himself. He makes everything the way it ought to be. What this means for those that trust in Jesus is that he will have a relationship with them. Just like super heroes do away with bad guys, so also Jesus will defeat all of the enemies to his kingdom.

PERSON B

Look what happens to these paper clips when they are

drawn to Jesus. They are also drawn to one another. This is what the Bible calls fellowship. The Greek word is koinonia. Can you say KOY-NO-NEE-UH? What that means is a "self-sacrificing con-formity to a shared vision". Those are big words, so let me explain.

SELF-SACRIFICING: Jesus comes before what everybody else wants to do. We give up our wants for Jesus.

CONFORMITY: Instead of our own wishes, we all do what Jesus says.

TO A SHARED VISION: Jesus is the shared vision. That means something that people share. It's like selling all of your stuff and giving all of your time to build a tree house with your friend.

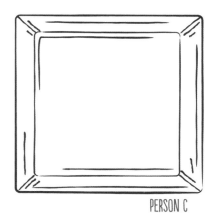

PERSON C

This means that the way you live with other people tells something about your love for Jesus. If you always put yourself and what you want first, it means that you think that you are more important than God and more valuable than Jesus' community. Sometimes people will hurt you within the church. Sometimes you will do something to hurt other people. We are a broken people. But we are a people that is being changed by Jesus. When you are drawn to Jesus you are drawn to other believers in Jesus too. Don't ever forget that!

Have you been drawn to Jesus and his church?

Do you love other people in the church? Do you love their ideas or just your own?!

NO LONGER ALIENS TO GOD

Today we get to learn a big word. It is the word reconciled. Being reconciled is what happens whenever two or more people who have been fighting and arguing decide to come back together. To reconcile something means to take two things that are far apart and to bring them together.

This verse in Colossians tells us that Jesus has reconciled us to God. That is really good news! But it also has some really bad news in it, too. In verse 21, it says that

TO LEARN WHAT ALIEN MEANS, LET'S SPEND A LITTLE TIME DRAWING A PICTURE OF OUR OWN ALIEN

we were "alienated" and "hostile in mind". Those are two words that we need to learn.

What makes him an alien? Is it that he is different? He isn't like us? That is what it kind of means that we were alienated from God. Because of our sin, we no longer look the way God created us to look. We are no longer at home in God's kingdom. We have placed ourselves outside of his loving rule. That is what it means that we are alienated.

It also says that we are "hostile in mind". Hostile is another word that means "angry" or "mad". Sin so messes up our hearts that we start to think that God is the bad guy in the story, and we are the good guy. We start hating God, and as a result of this we "do evil deeds". We do these "evil deeds" because we assume that our way is better than God's way.

Thankfully that is not all the Bible says. Verse 21 is the bad news, but verse 22 is the good news. He has reconciled us. That means that he changes our hearts and our minds. Sin separates us from God. It makes us aliens to him. But Jesus makes all things back to how they should be. And because of the work of Jesus, we will be presented to God "holy and blameless and above reproach before him". That is another way of saying that we will be clean before him, and that we will not have any sin that stands in the way of our relationship with God. Jesus has made the way for us to be reconciled with God. When we turn away from sin and trust in Jesus, then we are reconciled.

Thank God for reconciling people to Himself.

Have you been reconciled to God?

DON'T BE SHIFTY WITH YOUR HOPE IN JESUS

It's part of human nature to want to be on the winning team. We also like cheering for winning teams in sports. But not everyone can win. Some sports fans only like their team when they win and they stop cheering for them when they lose. At the beginning of the year these fans are sure that their team will be awesome. Then, with several losses in a row, their hope begins to shift. They quit cheering for their team. These fans are shifty in their hope.

God tells us in Colossians that our hope in Jesus should not be shifty. All of those great promises that we saw last time (that we are reconciled to God and made clean before Him) are only ours if we remain faithful to Jesus. We can't put a little bit of hope in Jesus and then "change our team" whenever things get tough.

There will be very difficult times in your life. There will be times when it seems like God is a million miles away. But everything that he does (even the painful stuff) is for our good. In the same way, there will be times in your life when everything is going wonderfully. It will seem like you have the blessings of heaven upon everything that you do. These times can actually be more dangerous than when things aren't going as well because we are more likely to forget God and his goodness.

No matter what happens in your life, always remain faithful to Jesus. There was a guy who lived a really long time ago named John Bunyan. He was going through some really difficult times (at one point he would actually have to go to jail for his faith in Jesus, but this story came well before that). Bunyan thought that he had lost his faith in Jesus. His faith was getting really weak (as all of ours will do at times). He was so worried and troubled that he went for a walk in a field. While going on his walk, a sentence came into his mind—"Your righteousness is in heaven, John". That reminded him that it was what Jesus had done that mattered and not how much faith he had. He realized that no matter if he was doing really well or really bad in his relationship with Jesus, he still belonged to Jesus and all the blessings of Christ where his. This helped him to hang on to Jesus.

Always hang on to Jesus.

Read Jude 24, and then thank God for his power to keep us from falling.

REJOICE IN SUFFERING?

LET'S BEGIN BY MAKING UP STORIES ABOUT THE WORST DAY WE'VE EVER HAD. I'LL TELL A STORY AND THEN YOU CAN TELL A STORY.

The apostle Paul had some pretty bad days in his life, too. One time some really mean people decided to beat him up. And then he had to go to jail for telling people about Jesus. The bad news doesn't end there, because while they were moving him to a new jail his ship wrecked! So, he was beat up, arrested, and then his ship wrecked.

When your ship wrecks you lose all of your stuff. They barely made it alive, and when they landed they were lost on an island. That'd be a really bad day, wouldn't it? But it doesn't stop there. Paul also got bitten by a snake when he landed. What a horrible day! So when Paul wrote things about "suffering" he knew what he was talking about. Suffering is having a really bad things happen to you. Paul put a surprising word in front of "sufferings" though. He wrote, "Rejoice in your sufferings." We would expect him to say, "get through" or "complain about" or "pray about"

your sufferings. He didn't. He said, "Rejoice in your sufferings". That means to take joy in them. To delight in them! How in the world can we do that?

There are a couple clues in Colossians 1:24-26 that help us see how Paul was able to rejoice in his sufferings and how we can, too.

FiRST, he loved the good news about Jesus and the church more than himself. He knew that his bad days could help other people come to know Jesus. And because he loved God, his gospel, and other people more than himself, Paul was able to go through a ton of bad stuff with joy. He knew that it would lead to other people finding joy in Jesus, and so that made him rejoice.

SECONDLY, Paul knew that it was God's plan for his life to go through bad things so that other people could know Jesus. We don't know what life has for us. We don't know for sure what God will call us to do. Sometimes we will have great days, and sometimes we will have bad days. We don't know when we wake up in the morning which day we get. But we *do* know that God is in charge of every day. Paul knew that God would never do anything mean to him, so it must be for his good and the good of other people.

How do you usually respond to bad things happening? Does this say anything about our hearts? Let's pray that the Lord would help us to suffer well when he calls us to suffer.

THE GREATEST MYSTERY EVER

Do you like mysteries? A mystery is whenever something is hidden and you have to figure it out through clues. Some mysteries are easy to solve. Others are really tough. Some mysteries are so great that they have to be solved for us by somebody else.

There was a mystery in the Bible, too. People in the Old Testament (that is the time before Jesus) only knew part of what God was going to do through Jesus. They only knew certain parts of the mystery. But as time kept marching forward, certain clues kept popping up. God left his fingerprints all over the Old Testament story. Now, we can look back (having discovered the mystery) and we can learn that Jesus is everywhere in the Old Testament story.

What is this greatest mystery ever? Paul says it is:

Christ in you, the hope of glory.

What does this mean? This is the answer to the greatest mystery ever. It means that God himself is going to live in our hearts. He is going to change us from the inside out. And the fact that we have Jesus in our hearts assures us that we will have a future life with him whenever he returns.

This was a great mystery because people thought that the Rescuer that was predicted in the Old Testament would be a really powerful leader. Don't get me wrong, Jesus is a powerful leader but not in the way that was expected. They figured he would be like a really powerful king with big muscles and good looks. They didn't expect the Rescuer to be God coming to earth as a baby. And they didn't expect him to come and die on a cross. Nor did they expect him to rise from the dead and then pour out his Spirit (that means come to live in our hearts) upon not only Jewish people but also those who weren't Jewish people.

All of the Bible point to Jesus. And it unwraps for us the greatest gift we are given. That gift is "Christ in you, the hope of glory". That's what Paul means when he says, "the riches of the glory of this mystery". Understanding this mystery only comes as God shows it to us.

Let's thank God for this mystery and pray that he continues to reveal it to our hearts every day.

Think of someone who doesn't know Jesus. Let's pray for him or her that God would show Jesus as the greatest treasure in life.

GOSPEL TOIL

You are called to give your life to hard work. The Bible speaks often of hard work. In the Old Testament, God tells us to look at ants. Let's read Proverbs 6 and also watch a video of ants. The point from Proverbs 6 is that ants are always working hard. Another word for their hard work is the word "toil". They work hard to provide for their families. Ants do hard things.

In Colossians 1:28-29, Paul reminds the Colossians that he works hard. He works hard to make sure that people understand who Jesus is and come to treasure him. Notice that Paul describes his work as, "struggling with all his energy that he powerfully works within me". Paul is not lazy and he works really hard. But he knows that it is God who is working within him. This means that we don't sit around and wait for a feeling before we start doing gospel work. We work hard knowing that the Lord is at work within us to "act and to will according to his good pleasure".

This video is informative about the hard work of ants: http://bit.ly/1iKXpDi

Field Notes

> WHAT ARE SOME EXAMPLES OF GOSPEL WORK?

THINGS THAT SHOW HOW AWESOME JESUS IS !

Many people give their life to work. That is certainly an honorable thing. But it's not the best thing. The best thing is to give your life to gospel work. That does not mean you have to be a preacher, worship leader, writer, or bible teacher. What it does mean is that whatever God gives you to do, you need to do it with all your energy (like the ant) for the purpose of making Jesus look good..

Let's thank God for those who have toiled to bring the gospel to us.

Pray also that God would show you the gospel toil that he wants you to do and that he gives you the strength to accomplish it.

TRADING TREASURE FOR MOWING SHOES

Did you know that some people teach things that are not true? Some do it by accident because they think what they are teaching is true. Others reject what God says and try to teach their own version of truth. That is what was happening in Colossae to the people who Paul wrote to. They were teaching people that if they wanted to have "full knowledge", then they needed to do certain things. They were making fun of the Colossians telling them they weren't good followers of Jesus—that they were just a bunch of empty-heads. They tried convincing the Colossians that what they really needed was to go through THEIR special program in order to have real knowledge.

Paul let the Colossians know that even though these false teachers sounded smart THEY were really the empty-heads. He did this by reminding all wisdom and knowledge comes from Jesus. Therefore, these false teachers were the silly ones. They were trying to encourage people to find "full knowledge" outside of Jesus. That's foolish because there is no knowledge outside of Jesus.

I think we can illustrate this using one of your favorite toys and an old lawn-mowing

*You'll need a little preparation for this one. Read through the lesson beforehand so you can be prepared with the "presents" for the illustration.

*It doesn't need to be an old lawn-mowing shoe. Use anything that would be a disappointing prize. It works best to have a pair of something, though, as you'll wrap the second one up into the shiny package.

shoe*. What is your favorite toy, right now?

I will trade you one of my old lawn-mowing shoes for your favorite toy. That means you won't get to play with it again because I'm going to sell it. But you will have my old shoe. Does that sound like a smart trade? You aren't going to make that deal are you? But this is exactly what the Colossians were doing.

We can look at this and say, "silly Colossians", but we do not understand how believable their arguments were. These false teachers sounded really smart. But, hey! I have another trade for you. In this beautiful box is an amazing present that is far cooler than your favorite toy. I'll trade you this for your favorite toy. Do you want to do this trade?

Do you see the difference? Sometimes false teaching is put into a really nice package, but it's just a big trick. The key to not making such silly trades is to be convinced that Jesus is enough. If you traded your favorite toy for this box, it was because you thought something might be better. It's not the same with Jesus—there is nothing better than Jesus. If you are convinced that you already have the greatest treasure in the world, then you won't be fooled into trading it for a lie. .

Thank God that Jesus is the greatest treasure. Is this great treasure yours?

NAILED TO THE CROSS

Why do people have to go to jail? Usually, they go to jail when they do bad things, and the judge sentences them to jail to pay for their crimes. That means that people answer to the laws of our country. If you break a law you must answer for it.

In the same way—actually in a much bigger way—we must answer to God. He created us. He made us to enjoy him and to extend his glory (that means to show everybody with how we live and love that God is amazing). Instead, we decided to enjoy ourselves and to extend our own glory (tell everybody how awesome we are). This is called rebellion. As a result of our rebellion, God punishes our sin.

This is what Paul was talking about in verse 13 when he says, "dead in your trespasses". A trespass means something that we do that is God doesn't like. What are a few things that you have done in your life that God doesn't like? I will share a few that I have done, too.

Some of my trespasses

_____   _____   _____

_____   _____   _____

_____   _____   _____

This is really sad news, but each of these make you (as mine make me) guilty before God. This is what Paul calls our "record of debt" in verse 14. The punishment for disobeying God is death. It is being separated from everything that is good, including God's good presence. That is really scary isn't it?

That'd be really horrible if we just went to bed right now without sharing the good news (that's what gospel means, by the way—"good news"). In verse 14 Paul wrote that Jesus "nailed these to the cross". When Jesus died on the cross, he took those things above and nailed them to a cross.

Some people have done this as an illustration. They have taken a sheet of paper and written down all of the sins that they could think of. And then they took a nail and a big wooden cross and went and nailed that sin upon the cross. That's a great way to remember it, but the truth is, Jesus is the one that nailed our sins to the cross. He took our sins and nailed them to the cross.

One of the things that Jesus said on the Cross as he was dying is "It is finished." What was finished? Jesus' work of taking my sins and yours and nailing it up to the Cross is what was finished. If we confess our sin to Jesus, he forgives us because it has been nailed to the cross!.

 **Thank God for his forgiveness in Jesus.**

DANCING WITH SHADOWS

COLOSSIANS 2:6-15

LET'S BEGIN BY WATCHING A VIDEO ON HOW TO MAKE SHADOW PUPPETS AND THEN WE'LL TRY OUR BEST TO MAKE SOME REALLY COOL ONES.

WHAT WAS YOUR FAVORITE SHADOW PUPPET?

Did you know that everybody makes a shadow? Let's look at your shadow on the wall and then my shadow on the wall. Shadows are cool, but are they accurate?

What are some things missing in your shadow?

_____

_____

_____

_____

_____

_____

This video shows how to make a few shadow puppets: http://bit.ly/17VOSvh

Wouldn't it be really silly if you and I went to hang out and the whole time I only hung out with your shadow? We would eat pizza, and I'd talk to your shadow and ask it how the pizza was. We'd play mini-golf, and when you made a good shot I'd try to give your shadow a high-five. The whole time I'd never talk to you, only your shadow. Wouldn't that be silly?

That is kind of what was happening at Colossae. There were many things in the Old Testament that were shadows of Jesus. They were things that were pointing to Jesus. They looked like Jesus, and they helped people sort of know what Jesus would be like—but they weren't Jesus. When Jesus came, it would be really dumb to still care about his shadow. But these guys were telling people to still do things as if Jesus hadn't come. You don't hang out with a shadow when the real thing is right before your eyes.

The false teachers tried convincing people that these "shadows" would keep them from sinning. God tells us that this is silly. "Things" cannot rescue us from our sin. Only a person can, and that person is Jesus. Only Christ can rescue us and "stop the indulgence of the flesh."

Let's thank God that he has given us the real thing in Jesus.

KEEPING YOUR EYES ON CHRIST

COLOSSIANS 2:16-23

THIS VIDEO OF USAIN BOLT'S WORLD RECORD 100M IS A GOOD ONE: HTTP://BIT.LY/LQUOUB

Let's begin by watching a couple videos of really fast runners in a race*. What do you notice about their heads? They don't look from side to side, do they? That is because runners are trained to keep their eye on the goal. If they start looking from side to side, it messes them up and slows them down.

What is one of the reasons why we might turn our heads in a race? We usually do that because we are afraid that somebody is going to catch them. But checking to see where your opponent is doesn't help you. It actually hurts you, because turning your head to the side makes you run slower. The best thing to do is keep your eyes on the finish line and run really fast.

The same thing is true in our life with Jesus. Sometimes we can get scared and start looking away from Jesus. Or other things can steal our attention and cause us to stop looking toward Christ. Here in Colossians 3, we are told to "seek the things that are above". That means to live our life for the things that will last forever.

Things that will not last forever:

_____   _____

_____   _____

_____   _____

Things that will last forever:

_____   _____

_____   _____

_____   _____

What really matters are the things that will last forever. That is the most important thing about us.

Therefore, as the old poem goes, "Only one life, will soon be past, only what's done for Christ will last."

Are you seeking the things that are above?

WEARING THE RIGHT CLOTHES

IT'S ALWAYS IMPORTANT TO WEAR THE RIGHT CLOTHES. LET'S SEE IF YOU CAN PICK THE RIGHT CLOTHES.

COLOSSIANS 3:1-4

Outside to play in the snow	Pajamas
Swimming in the summer	Helmet, gun, army gear
Playing baseball	Old clothes, shoes, pants
Going to a funeral	Winter coat, gloves, scarf, pants
Going to sleep	Helmet, pants, glove, t-shirt
Just hanging out	Tuxedo, dress shoes, a flower
Being in the army	Dress shirt, dress shoes, black tie
Playing basketball	Gym shorts, tennis shoes, b-ball shirt
At your wedding	Swimming trunks, sunscreen, sandals
Working a dirty job	Blue jeans, t-shirt, shoes, whatever

MATCH it!

ere in Colossians, Paul was reminding them that they had been changed by Jesus. Imagine if a baseball player who had been traded showed up at his new team wearing his old uniform. That'd be silly. He changed teams. That's what Paul was saying here to the Colossians. They had changed teams. Therefore, they no longer ought to wear their old uniform. Their old uniform was the things in verses 5-11. Their new uniform was the stuff in verses 12-17.

The way that you go about "putting on the right clothes" and "taking off the old clothes" is through staying focused on Jesus. When we are keeping our eyes on Jesus, it helps us to know what types of things are appropriate.

DOES SAYING MEAN THINGS TO PEOPLE LOOK LIKE JESUS?	YES	NO
DOES LOVING SOMEONE LOOK LIKE JESUS?	YES	NO
DOES BEING REALLY ANGRY AND ACTING OUT LOOK LIKE JESUS?	YES	NO
DOES FORGIVING SOMEONE LOOK LIKE JESUS?	YES	NO

It is because Jesus has given us a new life that we are able to look like him. As Christians we are called to look more like Jesus than the world.

What in your life doesn't look like Jesus? How does that change? What does look like Jesus?

OBEY EVEN WHEN IT'S TOUGH

If I told you that you had to eat your favorite food would you whine and cry and complain? Probably not, because that would be an order that is easy to obey. But what if I told you that you had to eat your least favorite food? That would be a little more difficult to obey wouldn't it?

Obeying Jesus can be like that. Sometimes we are called to do things in our relationships with other people that we don't necessarily like. But what God teaches us in these verses is that there is a certain way that we are to act in our relationships with other people. And we are to do this even whenever it is difficult.

God has lovingly put people in charge of you. Sometimes these people will ask you to do things that you may not like doing (like eating your least favorite food). Even parents have people that they have to obey—and sometimes we don't like the rules either. But God calls us to obey them out of a love for him. When we obey those

Field Notes

> WHAT IS YOUR FAVORITE FOOD?

> WHAT IS YOUR LEAST FAVORITE FOOD?

that lovingly lead us we are saying that we agree with how God has set up his world.

There is one other thing that is really cool in these verses. God doesn't just talk to the kids. He also talks to the fathers. He tells them what kind of dads they should be to their children. And this also helps us to know that both kids and their parents answer to God. He is the one that is in charge of everyone. This means that even if your parent asks you to do something that is sin, then you should listen to God.

It is hard work being a kid. It is also hard work being a parent. Thankfully, Jesus gives us grace for the times when we mess up. He also gives us the power to joyfully obey even when we might rather do things our own way.

What do you think is the hardest thing about being a parent? Discuss the difficulties of being a parent with your child. Also discuss the joys of being a parent.

What do you think is the hardest thing about being a kid? Discuss the difficulties that you remember with being a kid. Also discuss the joys of being a kid.

Thank God for the relationships that he has given us.

KNOCK! KNOCK!

BEGIN BY TAKING TURNS TELLING KNOCK-KNOCK JOKES.*

When you knock on a person's door you are asking them to open the door and let you into their lives—even if in a small way. What happens if you knock on the door and nobody answers? It might mean that nobody is home. Or it could be that someone is home but they do not want to talk to you. Either way when we knock on the door of a home we hope that the person is there and will open the door to us.

As Paul closes his letter to the Colossians he has a prayer request. He asks his friends to pray that people would open up their doors for his message about Jesus. What Paul is praying for is a chance to share the good news of Jesus with many people. We should pray this same thing for ourselves and for other followers of Jesus. We should pray that God gives us opportunities to tell the good news of His Son. Other people need to know what you've learned about God from Paul's letter to the Colossians. They too need to know that Jesus is all that they need.

While Paul encourages the Colossians to pray for opportunities to share the gospel with people, he also

These are some pretty good ones and age appropriate: http://lajollamom.com/2011/07/kid-friendly-knock-knock-jokes/ Be sure to research the knock-knock jokes before you simply go searching on the internet, not all of them are clean.

reminds them to speak with grace towards people. In fact he tells them to make their language seasoned with salt. We use salt sometimes to make our food taste better. Paul is telling us to think about the way that we talk to people. Just like salt makes food taste better, we want to make sure that our words help people to see how beautiful Jesus is.

As we close out our journey through Colossians let's review some of the things that we've learned and that we can share with other people.

Things I've learned from Colossians and can share with other people:

_____   _____

_____   _____

_____   _____

Pray for opportunities to tell people about the good news of Jesus

Pray that other missionaries will get opportunities to tell people about Jesus

Thank God for his letter to the Colossians and all that you've learned

Additional Resources

* Arnold, Clinton E. The Colossian Syncretism: The Interface between Christianity and Folk Belief at Colossae. Grand Rapids, MI: Baker Books, 1996.

* Bruce, F. F. The Epistles to the Colossians, to Philemon, and to the Ephesians. Grand Rapids, Mich: W.B. Eerdmans, 1984.

* Garland, David E. Colossians and Philemon. Grand Rapids, Mich: Zondervan Pub. House, 1998.

* Moo, Douglas J. The Letters to the Colossians and to Philemon. Grand Rapids, Mich: William B. Eerdmans Pub. Co, 2008.

* O'Brien, Peter Thomas. Colossians, Philemon. Waco, Tex: Word, 1982.

* Storms, C. Samuel. The Hope of Glory: 100 Daily Meditations on Colossians. Wheaton, Ill: Crossway Books, 2007.

* Vaughan, Curtis. Colossians and Philemon. Grand Rapids, Mich: Zondervan Pub. House, 1980.

* Wright, N. T. The Epistles of Paul to the Colossians and to Philemon: An Introduction and Commentary. Leicester, England: Inter-Varsity Press, 1988.

* http://www.monergism.com/topics/sermon-manuscripts-mp3s-scripture/colossians

More from Mike Leake

TORN TO HEAL

31 DAYS OF PRAYING FOR YOUR WIFE

31 DAYS OF PRAYING FOR YOUR SON

31 DAYS OF PRAYING FOR YOUR DAUGHTER

PRAYING FOR PURITY

FOLLOW MIKE ON
HIS BLOG, BORROWED LIGHT

WWW.MIKELEAKE.NET

Made in the USA
Lexington, KY
05 July 2015